Jon Burgerman

Pens are my Friends

Hello there, thanks for buying this book.
If you are reading this book in a shop and
mulling over whether to buy it or not I'd advise
that you do. No-one else will want it now you've
put your greasy finger prints all over it.

This book collects a lot of my work from the last
seven years or so. Of course, not everything I've
worked on during this time has made it in and
some really nice things had to be left out but
generally this should give you an overview of
some of the projects, ideas and exhibitions I've
completed. Oh and meals I've scoffed.

Looking over all the work I can't help thinking
a couple of things; Firstly, I must have gone
through a lot of pens (I always feel a little bad
when throwing them away) and secondly, maybe
I should get out more and doodle less. I don't
have much else to write, the work should speak
for itself really, plus I wrote all of the captions
through-out the book (which should act as a little
running commentary) and that took ages and
now I'm all typed-out and in need of a nap.

contents ⚡

doodled since
day one
essay

Always a professional, Jon gave me a concise brief when he asked me if I'd contribute a text for this book. He offered a clear desire and few, if any limitations. Saying he figured there was enough explanation about him in this book already, he expressed a wish for a line that might locate him amongst his creative influences and pay due respects. This respect due to a life's work more so than it may be awarded to any general aesthetic or specific contribution. A love for Picasso cannot be dwindled down to political appreciation for the gesture of Guernica or any foreray into cubism or lust. What Jon requested reveals as much about his work as the work itself. It speaks towards something more important than he is. For lack of some huge dominating word, this important thing is 'whatever' he has in common with other people. So this is where we'll eventually go.

Jon never mentioned the word Doodle, but like a dudeltopf this is where I'll stop before that. For what it is worth, Wikipedia does have a section on Doodling, and Jon is listed there with Serge Aragonés of Mad Magazine fame. If we sketched Doodling into a family tree, it could be the cousin of comics, the child of activism, and the nephew of Graffiti (an uncle who encouraged it to sneak out of the house at night and acquire a shared addiction to big walls and the adrenaline rush of personal risk). A doodle is defined as an unfocused drawing, which is made almost subconsciously; the mind preoccupied or struggling to deny distraction. A doodle takes shape in the void, finding form from the shadows. Now a 'thing,' doodle was previously a verb. You could say that Homer Simpson has doodled America into laughing at narratives many viewers might normally find outrageous. D'oh! Keep drinking Duffs. Words change with time and today, doodling appears as a fashion, but also as an emotionally informed approach to media aesthetics. Doodle as defense.

Doodling may evolve into practices of calligraphy, character design, typography and all sorts of visual sounds. It follows flow and challenges direction giving it full zeitgeist credibility. At a time when no authority is left to believe and conspiracy has stepped out of the closet, doodling deconstructs the almighty POINT. In a doodle, having a point is useless as each point becomes a series of dots submerged and overshadowed by process until any first conclusions are suffocated. The line follows itself. Passing and wasting time unite to overthrow judgment in the production line. When this so-called point of most stories appears to be completely subjective, and way too often appears to be too forced, this is refreshing. It may even be vital at a time when politics is only another form of entertainment and every authority offers its own reasons not to be trusted.

Though Jon has earned recognition as one of the fathers of a so called Doodle movement (and the character revolution that has been holding its hand), a father is always a son, and a grandson, and an ex-boyfriend and so on and this sort of reference should remind us that he's just a young man. In mentioning his influences, Jon jumps from Phil Frost to Mr. Jago of the Scrawl Collective and from Basquiat to Barry McGee. He mentions Paul Smith, David Carson and Dave the Chimp and, while people will forever discuss their individual merits, there is something underlying that all of these inspirational talents share.

Burgerman belongs to a generation of artists whose practice is both influenced and informed by Graffiti, comics and their offspring. Graffiti because of its bravery and authenticity, its struggle for style and the positive nature of its violent modern birth; and comics, because, they were everywhere in our western pop lives (cereal boxes, Saturday morning cartoons and so forth) and yet, from Superman to the Simpsons they have managed to remain the only accepted media vehicle (aside from so-called art) to deliver news too real for the 11 o'clock broadcast and packed chock full of opinions that could not be proven right or wrong, but made certain sense. The connection is not spray-paint or style or sarcasm. It isn't Spy vs. Spy or something from Hannah Barbara. It can't be flossed out of a character's three teeth. It is not about branding oneself or just writing your name. It has little to do with laws or preconceived public perception. It shares influences, but also imaginative drive. It is about art and forgets art. Reflective of this moment in history, it values evolution over revolution and shares a desire to show things as they are. As they are, but where are they? Where is Jon?

To locate Jon, and many of what he called his 'artist wise likes', we can look at locations. So simple. On public walls and screens, product packaging and Playstations; on surfboards, skateboards, trains, guitars, clothes and into characters, his work finds its way into every crack in the cultural sphere. It is democratic without trying to be or talking about it. This speaks of both engagement as a person and the heart of a practice, a diverse shared curiosity that has purpose extending past all those laughable points. It speaks of collaboration, which means it speaks of love. With love it speaks of practice.

When Jon told me that for him seeing Basquiat's work was like a light bulb going off, he didn't refer to one project, but to the artist's ability to experiment on so many different levels and remain relevant in each of them. Basquiat went for a complete remixing of mediums and recycling of stale realities. Jon's work shares this excitement, becoming an exploration of movement; lines latching onto various vessels and leading their own lives. There is no snobbery, just well versed creative action. Only experience is sacred and this action itself is the ambition. This is a casual betrayal of art's elitist history (coupled with all other elitist histories), which is a common sentiment amongst Jon's peers. As American artist Jeremy Fish puts it:

Harlan Levey
Harlan Levey is the Editor in Chief of Modart Magazine and the co-founder of the No New Enemies network.

Born in 1974, Harlan lives in Brussels, Belgium.

Modarteurope.com
Nonewenemies.net
Egs.edu

"Throughout the ages people have tried to confine art to movements so they could discuss it over wine and cheese and try to make more relevance out of something than it needs. In art school I was repeatedly told that art is a language of communication and that you're supposed to use these tools to tell the world something and make it a better place. For me, if you're just throwing your stuff in galleries, you're communicating with an audience that can afford to be a part of that and at that point you've really levelled out anybody who doesn't have the money to be part of that."

Let loose. Wherever and whenever you feel like it. Love. Experiment. Fail. Fail better. Pay attention and keep a thousand grains of salt in your pocket. There is a nonchalant rejection of authority and greying structures, characteristic of that movement that we cannot yet (or I will not yet) name and yet both Fish and Burgerman belong to. We can link it to Keith Haring's love for large murals. The first images I saw of his work were on the Berlin Wall. From there we can tie it to light and look at the essence of why activists like Abbie Hoffman and artists like Basquiat chose to share their voices at street level where an artist is an activist and vice versa. Where a person is a person. Open source and peer to peer. Subject, not predicate. What art can mean in a life. Basquiat once said, "I don't think about art when I'm working. I try to think about life."

When Jon lists Adam Neate amongst his 'artist wise likes', I'm not sure if it is for the skilful technique and thoughtful poetry in his portraits, or the way Adam continues to distribute his work for free to as many people as possible. Continues to do this even as informed collectors wince while their possessions become less rare. Less valuable? Not for anybody who is paying attention. Not in an emotional economy, the one proper to this thing called art. We could doodle this genealogy through the roots of Dada and Surrealism, Low Brow and Sketchbook, into, over and under anything that was initially rejected as art, referring instead to the influences of experience and the struggle, as Jeremy Fish said, to make things just a bit better.

Of course this better is vague. This does not make it less important. While Burgerman's lines bend into playful and even positive forms, this does not mean they are fuelled by optimism. Just as in graffiti culture, where the line takes a stance and the flavour is to slice through it all, cut through the layers and destroy things with a single macho line; destruction is not necessarily negative. To many, this was making things better.

Burgerman also noted Cy Twombly and Jim Avignon as inspirations and we can imagine that like Jon, Jim might have seen the Kentucky legend in the scratches on the bottom of a skateboard. Though his work can be discussed within the dimensions of historic graffiti, etches, and scrawls, Mr. Twombly himself has nothing to do with the culture surrounding Graffiti today. But if a doodle is a point of departure, I'll jump to Avignon's name and a Twombly victory: October 2007, Avignon, France and Twombly's work is on display to the delight of a crowd brought together by art collector Yves Lambert. Shortly after, French courts would hear of an act of vandalism that occurred at the exhibition. A young woman gave a lipstick kiss to the white of a painting called Phaedrus. Vandalism? For the collector the painting was ruined, its value diminished. Yet if we are to accept the alleged vandal's claim that it was an amorous act of spontaneity, that she'd been called to the kiss, then perhaps she was correct in saying that the artist would understand.

If we accept this, then even if we reduced his life to this very instant, Twombly would have succeeded in sharing the practice of love. Bright red cherry on frosty white, Phaedrus was after all written on the question of how love should be practised. In my eyes, her action gave 'added value,' which is after all what all enterprise seeks these days. What does this change? Everything and nothing. It is useless. Maybe this makes it art.

Twombly managed to provoke the same silly question as all illicit public actions: Is it art or is it vandalism? The incident reveals that the answer depends on the person you are asking, more so than it does the art. The answer has nothing to do with the art. It is a distant predicate, brought to proximity through speculation. This is a movement doodling doesn't stop for. Doodling is all about the art, about the imagination. This is what differentiates it from sketching, scribbling and a host of other pregnant words. In many ways it is the embodiment of the 'whatever' Italian philosopher Giorgio Agamben promotes in his political interrogation of aesthetics in his work, "the Coming Community". Doodling is somehow a singularity that does not need definition. It is not 'whatever', like shrug your shoulders, don't give a fuck, numb whatever. It is 'whatever' as in whatever it is and will be. It is potential and care, not simply fatalistic Que sera sera. Agamben points out, that we don't love our girlfriend (for example), because she has long hair, nice lips or sings like a bird; it isn't this or that property that compels love. It isn't being Italian or Muslim, short or slender. Its love for a subject; first hand experience of what is (whatever it may be), before allowing the prejudice of predicate to colour the interaction. It is a general desire, which occurs prior to particular desire. He could be speaking about a doodle when he states that if human beings, 'were or had to be this or that substance, this or that destiny, no ethical experience would be possible... This does not mean, however, that humans are not, and do not have to be, something, that they are simply consigned to nothingness and therefore can freely decide whether to be or not to be, to adopt or not to adopt this or that destiny (nihilism and decisionism coincide at this point). There is in effect something that humans are and have to be, but this is not an essence nor properly a thing: It is the simple fact of one's own existence as possibility or potentiality... '

Though he begins with the space for potential, stating that the being of the future, 'the coming being,' is 'whatever being,' in a manner so wound in poetry that it seems like a useless political whine, by the time he wraps it up, there is an informed and wiry militancy to the claim that:

'Whatever singularity, which wants to appropriate belonging itself, its own being-in-language, and thus rejects all identity and every condition of belonging, is the principle enemy of the State. Wherever these singularities peacefully demonstrate their being in common there will be a Tiananmen, and, sooner or later, the tanks will appear.'

And here, in singular undefined resistance, where love is directly engaged with imagination and this vague sense of something better is essential, that Burgerman and his influences align themselves and begin to doodle in this spirit of a community to come, one without proper papers or specific aims. For better and for boredom, a doodle is a love song.

1
Interview with HL/Big Geezers DVD, 2008

2
http://en.wikipedia.org/wiki/Jean-Michel_Basquiat

3
Agamben, Giorgio, Michael Hardt (Translation). The Coming Community. Theory Out of Bounds, Vol. 1. University of Minnesota Press. Minneapolis, March 1993, 105 pages, Paperback, ISBN: 0816622353.

ornament is crime
essay

We all doodle. Starting at an early stage with various crayons, pens and pencils, a lot of enthusiasm but no sense for shapes whatsoever, we continue to refine our craft at every occasion and on any available surface: walls, exercise books, school tables, toilets. However, at a certain point during our lifetime the majority of us stop. Since mobile phones have liberated us from a fixed position while engaging in distant communication, the last refuge of adult doodling, the memo pad next to the phone is about to disappear from our homes.

Some may actually welcome this development. "Ornament is crime!" as the Austrian architect Alfred Loos put it in the early 20th century, further proclaiming, "The evolution of culture marches with the elimination of ornament from useful objects". But there is still some resistance. A generation of artists, designers and illustrators continues to leave their marks on every given object, be it paper, a wall, sneakers or customisable collector toys. One of them even successfully claims to be Mr. Hello Doodle himself! The shapes Jon Burgerman continuously produces are endless variations on how to establish an anthropomorphic gestalt from what is nothing more than the trace of a pen. By now, no object or media seems to be safe from his abstract patterns, recognizable characters and distinct drawing style, preferably without discontinuing the pen's flow once.

It makes total sense that Jon is from England, the country that set off the industrial revolution. Historically, doodling is unthinkable without that radical change in the means of production. Drawing and painting were no longer reserved to the aristocracy and their court painters, who up to then made exclusive use of feathers and Indian ink or fine hairbrushes and pigments. As another output from industrial manufactories, the pencil invaded the homes and lives of an emerging middle class suddenly empowered to their own creativity. Towards the end of the 19th century, drawing was established as a school subject and every adolescent was invited to awake his inner artist - or feel the frustration of lacking any talent. Soon modernity opened a niche for the synthesis of both: the dilettante claimed his share of the art market and, inspired by natives, naïves and lunatics, found ways to express intuitive creativity.

Jon is a great grandson of this artistic liberation. He started doodling before even being able to walk and has continued ever since. While others were engaged in ordinary teenage fun, Jon remained stoic and focused. Turning to his twenties, he continued to propel his therapeutic scribbles, meanwhile depictions of boys and girls with an irritated look in their misplaced eyes. In the 1990s, another technological paradigm marked its impression on the world of images: the digital. Pixel and vector creatures with wide shiny eyes and optimistic smiles had their explosive emergence around the turn of the millennium, with the first wave of the commercial Internet. Unimpressed by this digital revolution, Jon kept on doodling.

By doing so, he emerged as one of the protagonists of the parallel world of outsider art that has gained a remarkable recognition in recent years. Not being satisfied by the sterile aura of perfection the digital images radiate, the instant release of the pen following the curved line of the doodle proves to be the remedy for an increasing number of adherents. Artists and designers, all making perfect use of their computer, turn back to their sketchbooks. The digital is not used as a tool, but rather as a possibility to create creative networks, collaboration and co-operation.

Yet while more and more happy scribble and doodle creatures are born into our visual world, Jon's characters seem not to have lost the unsettled expression in their eyes. They continuously transmit an aura of being slightly out of place. This is not a question of lack of craftsmanship, as Jon shows a very distinct sense for the rules of design. It is a strategy to bring life to the surfaces his characters are bound to. As it is their fate to be flat, they cannot reach out but have to stretch and loll upon their 2D plane.

If ornament is a crime, Jon's work escapes any trial, breaking with its ornamental quality at the same time as fulfilling it. And while his characters' eyes look at us, they remind us to remain stoic and focused.

Peter Thaler & Lars Denicke
Pictoplasma.com
Peter Thaler studied film and worked as a freelance director for live action and animation projects. Frustrated by the main-stream animation industry's lack of appealing characters, Peter Thaler launched the Pictoplasma project in 1999 as a research tool for daring and stylistically outstanding characters in other fields: design, graphics, digital media, fine and urban art, plush dolls and urban vinyl toys. The project soon received international recognition with its growing online archive and best selling encyclopaedic publications.

Coming from a background of philosophy and cultural studies, Lars Denicke joined Peter to initiate the first ever Pictoplasma Conference in the year 2004. The event brought together a growing scene of leading artists and upcoming designers from various fields, all joined by the common interest for contemporary character design. From there on, Pictoplasma has curated a series of exhibitions, conferences and festivals, installations and performances all around the globe.

inky thumbs

print illustrations

Colourful print commissions from magazines to posters, stickers & packaging.

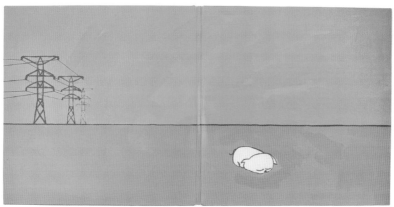

Charles Webster
One of the very first commissions I received was to paint a cover for the Charles Webster album Born on the 24th of July.

A few years later a remix LP of Charles' critically acclaimed album was released. I drew the little fella from the original cover having a go at remixing a track on his laptop.

1

2

3

4

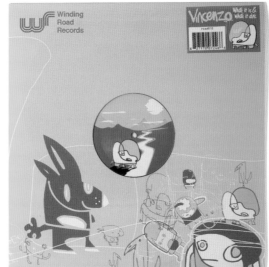

5

6

7

8

9

10

11

12

13

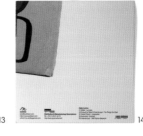

14

15

1–15
House Music
Interest for other house music labels followed the success of the cover for Charles Webster, including Winding Road Records (1–11) and Sushitech (12–15).

16
Me For Rent
Italian punk band Me For Rent saw these covers and asked me to personally create artwork for them. The bass player subsequently had a tattoo of one of the skulls put on his arm. Most of the band have one on them now.

17
Haphazard
Album cover for Rogue Audio's Haphazard.

16

17

Ninteenseventythree
Wrapping paper and greeting cards including seasonal Xmas designs, produced by Ninteenseventythree. Sold all over the world and often bought by savvy students as cheap posters.

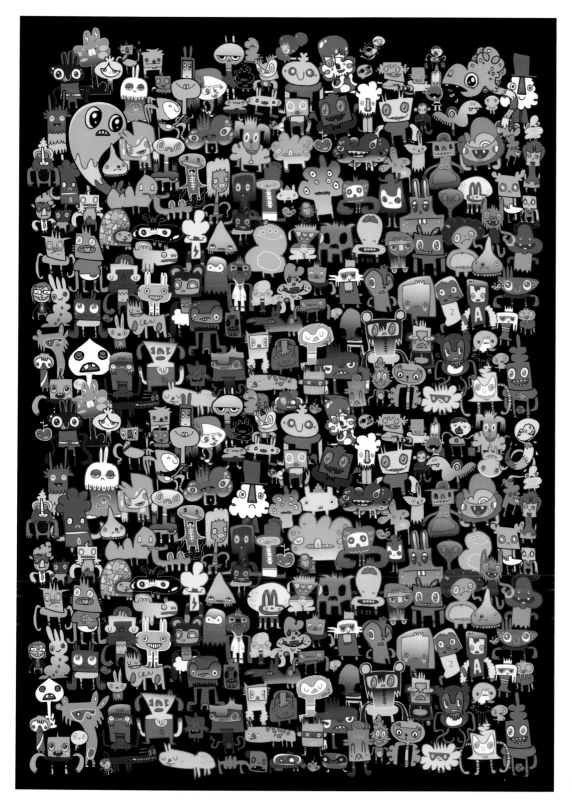

More wrapping paper designs
for Ninteenseventythree.

1

2

3

4

1&2
Freaky People
Pieces for an open air exhibition
in St. Petersburg, Russia.

3&4
Dreams and Nightmares
Pieces for 'Dreams and Nightmares'
show at the LCB Depot, Leicester.

5
Candy Poster
Poster made for SweetTalk,
Candy Collective's live lecture
program in Dublin. A video of
the talk is on the DVD.

1

JON BURGERMAN _132

2

3

4

1&2
ROJO Magazine
Spreads from ROJO®Seis.

3&4
Tiny Showcase
Two limited edition prints on 310gsm
acid-free Hahnemühle German
Etching Paper with UltraChrome ink.
Commissioned by Tiny Showcase
based in America.

SL Magazine
Monthly illustrations for
SL Magazine, South Africa.

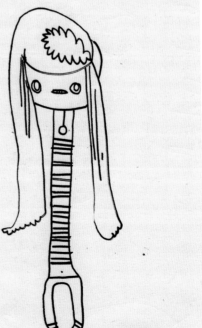
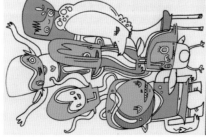

Celeste Magazine
Doodles about girls (not that I
understand much about them)
for Celeste Magazine, Mexico.

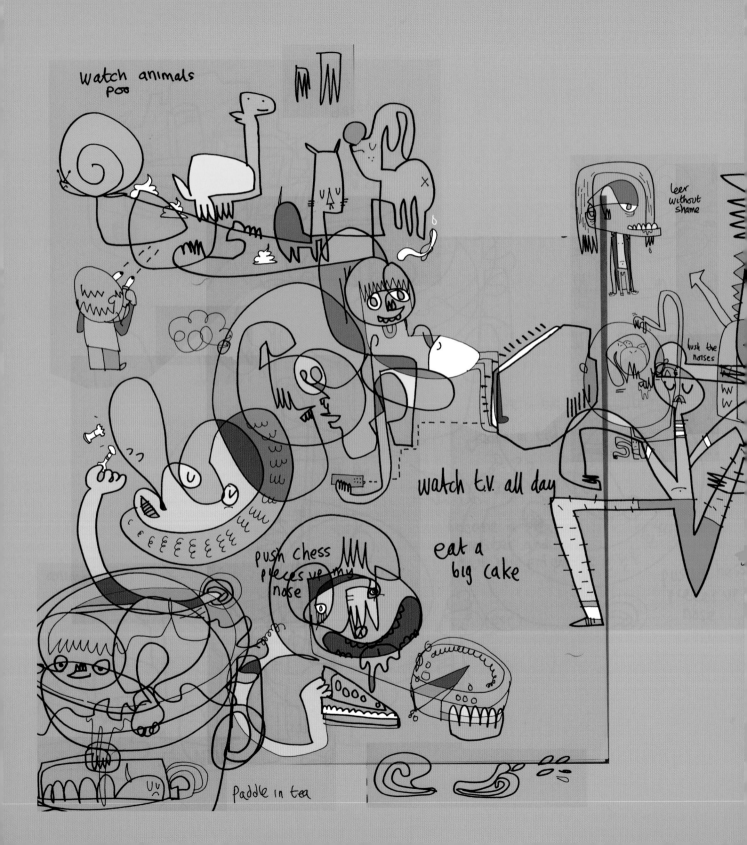

Watch animals
poo

leer
without
shame

hush the
noises

watch t.v. all day

push chess
pieces up my
nose

eat a
big cake

paddle in tea

Frivolous Pursuits
Sketchbook style artwork for the
second 'If I Could' book, which
invites artists to answer the
question; If you could do anything
tomorrow, what would it be?

1

2

1
Fingers and Thumbs
Black and red screen print.

2
Doomsday
Spread for Faesthetic Magazine.

3
Pocketless
Large printed canvas artwork
sold exclusively through
Blaugallery.com

1
Rainbow Chicken
Cover for Blowback Magazine.

2&3
High Score (2), Pong Kong (3)
Canvas prints for the video game
inspired 'I AM 8-BIT' group exhibition
at Gallery 1988, Los Angeles.

4&5
Wonderland Magazine
Illustrations about strange international
words, for Wonderland Magazine.

2

CERONE
(ITALIAN) EXCESSIVE MAKE-UP APPLIED

KAMAEIEIA
(GILBERTESE) TO WEAR A GARMENT 'TILL IT IS IN TATTERS

BUDDI
(TAMIL) SOMEONE WHO WEARS THICK GLASSES

COWICHAN
(BRITISH COLUMBIA, CANADA) A VIVIDLY PATTERNED SWEATER

TAN
(CHINESE) TO WEAR NOTHING ABOVE ONE'S WAIST

PADELLA
(ITALIAN) THE OILY STAIN ON CLOTHES

4

3

RIKURUTO-KATTO
(JAPANESE) A SHORT HAIRCUT TO IMPRESS PROSPECTIVE EMPLOYERS

EMBASAN
(MAGUINDANAON, PHILIPPINES) TO BATHE CLOTHED

JORGS [SCOTS]
THE NOISE OF SHOES WHEN FULL OF WATER

HACHIMAKI
(JAPANESE) HEADBANDS WORN BY MALES TO ENCOURAGE CONCENTRATION AND EFFORT

LIEBESTOETER
(GERMAN) UNATTRACTIVE UNDEWEAR

WO-KÛS-I-ÛK
(MALISEET, CANADA) A NECKLACE OF CLAWS

5

1
IndieCade
Poster and art print (both at
the same time) for 'IndieCade:
The International Festival of
Independent Games' at Open
Satellite 2008.

2–8
The Guild
Artwork made for the limited
edition Australian magazine The
Guild, produced by Andy Sargent.

2

3

4

5

6

7

8

1
Computer Arts Projects
Cover for an issue where three different illustrators were given the same briefs.

2
Computer Arts Projects
Cover for an issue about character design.

3
Computer Arts
Street scene of London for a 'design a taxi' competition spread.

4–6
Digit Magazine
Cover and inside spread about illustration heaven... and hell.

7&8
Digital Arts Magazine
Cover and inside spread for a feature about character creation.

happy illo angel

tag

monsters/
illustrators
'hell'

INSPIRATION FOR DIGITAL CREATIVES

FREE CD! CS3 TRAINING

Digital Arts

The world's biggest creative design & technology magazine

Character creation

Design award-Winning Character art

DESIGN FANTASY
Create this stunning fantasy art scene in Adobe Photoshop

T-SHIRT ART Illustrator design
Design a fresh summer character in Adobe Illustrator and then print it out as a T-shirt design

VECTOR PATTERNS Board art
Make brilliant skateboard designs using chaotic Illustrator patterns

VISUAL FX TV bumper design
Motion masterclass in After Effects for creating gripping 3D TV idents

Missing CD? Contact your newsagent

www.digitalartsonline.co.uk DEAD 2007 £5.99

9 771461 381038 2 7

Shoot from the hip
8 compact cameras
TESTED: the latest digital compact cameras delivering high-res photos

Accelerated 3D FX
Colin McRae DIRT
Exclusive making-of the cool Colin McRae CG game trailer

Hot! Photoshop CS3
Our in-depth review
It's here – the final release of Photoshop CS3 fully tested

7

People skills

Designing characters can be as lucrative as it is fun. Digital Arts found out how to give your creations a life of their own.

8

1

2

1&2
Luvgalz
Two prints made for the Paris
based exhibition 'Luvgalz'.

3
Clash
Giant A0 poster, commissioned
for 'Clash: An exhibition of
contemporary art from Birmingham
and West Midlands'. The posters
were pasted up around the city
of Birmingham and left to endure
the elements.

1

2

3

4

GET INVOLVED

FREE ENTRY
4 January 2007 7pm-12 midnight
The Social, 5 Little Portland Street, London W1
Special guest Leo the Wizard helped start Get Involved. So it's with smiles on their faces and love in their hearts that hosts G the P and Grandmaster Nolan welcome him behind the decks to spread his musical magic with them. What will they play? Anything you can shake your tailfeather to, of course!

Poster by JonBurgerman.com

5

6

7

1
Son of Rambow
Image for promotional use of the British film 'Son of Rambow', which is set in the 1980's when two boys watch a pirate copy of First Blood on video.

2&4
Arkitip
Hand painted envelope, posted to and then printed in Arkitip Magazine.

3
Sushi9
Playing card illustration for the project Sushi9.

5
Get Involved
Poster for the London music night.

6&7
ROJO® Berg
These pieces appeared in ROJO® Magazine.

8
Sony Advert
Advert of a family of freaks using Sony products outside.

8

X-CUP

2006 july no.1

●X-TOUCH 我的第一次 ●X-ROCK 海洋音樂祭 ●X-MARKET 創意市集 ●X-GRAFFITI 城市塗鴉人 ●X-FUNSer 放肆小子

非常公仔・第一次・紅色海洋搖滾不死・塗鴉人

by Jon Burgerman (UK)

ISSN 1819-4494

9 771819 449007 07

X-CUP NO.01　NT100

1
XFUNS Magazine
Customised wooden 'X-FUNSer'
for gala in Taiwan, organised
by XFUNS magazine.

2
Two Faced
Portrait of artist and toy designer
Nathan Jurevicius for the Two
Faced book and exhibition project.
In return Nathan drew me as
a grumpy and stoned tea pot.
Thanks Nathan.

2

4

5

6

7

8

9

10

11

12

1–3
Levis
Painted leatherette patches
commissioned for Levis 150th
Birthday of the 501s.

4–12
Mini Canvases
Printed canvases featuring
various characters.

Green Flutter (4), Anton (5),
Buggles (6), Purple (7), Stereoo (8),
Pinkturd (9), Zippy Blue (10),
Gumps (11), Ted (12).

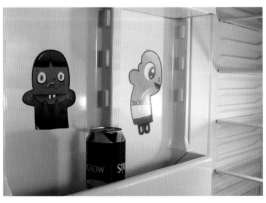

1–3
HA-HA Chaps
Repealable wall vinyls produced
by Pop Cling.com

4
Kingdrips
Wall vinyls for Kingdrips.

4

Banquet of Freeloaders
Wallpaper produced
by Maxalot.com

1

2

3

4

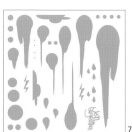

5

6

7

1–7
Adventures on Doodle-Safari 1&2
Wall vinyls produced by Domestic.fr

8
One Hundred Blurs
Specially invited commission
for the 100th issue of Blonde
Magazine, Germany.

1
Golden Time
Piece for IdN's Tiger Translate
Gold book.

2
**Fifth-teen Years
in Fifth-teen Seconds**
Artwork about accelerated time
for IdN's 15th anniversary book.

2

1
Women
One of four large scale posters made for a book on the theme of Women.

2
Strong Arms
A design for a screen printed poster, made out of sketchbook notes and drawings.

2

1
Donuts Party
Canvas print for the group
exhibition 'Donuts Party'
organised by Delkographik.

2
Print Commission

Duudles and Burgers
Pen pals lost in a duudle-warp

In 2003 Jon and Sune began sending each other silly doodles via email. It started like any polite talk:
  "Hello, would you like a cup of viridian doodle?"
  "Ah, much obliged. Would you, in return,
   like a sliced plate of scribbles?"
  "Oh, very tasty. Why don't you try this veggie burger?"

On and on it went, until one day in 2004 they decided to put the doodles, or the duudles, as they were now called, into a little concertina book entitled Hello Duudle.

The book was based on the style and general feel of the email ping-pong; playful, colourful and silly. Jon and Sune made the book without ever meeting up for real. Jon, being a vegetarian, in Nottingham and Sune living in Denmark, where bacon grows on trees. The cultural differences were vast. Also, Jon had a beard.

Despite all this they nevertheless managed to continue spitting out duudles, arm in arm, under the name Hello Duudle. Posters, stickers, exhibitions. You name it, the duudle empire was expanding.

Allow me at this juncture, to spend some words on the subject of Duudleville and the duudles. Duudleville, a pulsating and vibrant place, where the streets are paved with live dung beetles, causing your average insectophobe to have a hard time getting around. Home of the Duudles. This energetic, yet wee, line of species.

Yes, this is where they all go - the doodles. All of the carelessly thrown away scribbles you do whilst on the phone with your Mother-In-Law.

In 2006 another book was published; Hello Duudle - The Duudleville Tales, with the rather time consuming, yet greatly silly, element of one hand drawn duudle per book. A total of 1,000 duudles were drawn and tucked in with each copy. 'Lost Duudles' were their names, which is apt as the factory originally lost a few hundred of them meaning more had to be hastily scrawled.

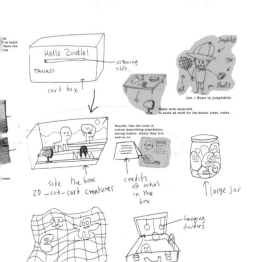

People investing in the book and consequently receiving a 'Lost Duudle' were asked to adopt the wee creature, name it and take a picture of it in its new found surroundings and send in a small report to the Hello Duudle site.

Theoretically each owner of Hello Duudle - The Duudleville tales were now able to see who else owned a copy, where they lived and which Lost Duudle they fed and made a bed for every night. Jon and Sune still hadn't met in real life.

In 2006 Pictoplasma asked the two Hello Duudlers to quit messing about and meet up for heaven's sake. The excuse they made up for this clashing of duudlers was to draw together all over a perfectly innocent gallery in England. The Colouring Room (see page 238) was what Pictoplasma fittingly decided to call this extravagancy into the world of duudles. After three days of constant duudling under the influence of strong tea and two iPods oozing out the best of duudley music (Jon surprising Sune with his music for slugs and Sune mesmerizing Jon with Danish elevator music) an entire room was duudled over. When the gallery opened every visitor was invited to fill in the Hello Duudles with sparkling colours.

Peterborough's finest bed & breakfast facilities hosted the two gents. Each morning Jon and Sune entertained each other with amusing tales from their respective rooms. For instance, Sune had a one square meter sized bathroom with two inch thick, red, carpet on the floor. Nothing better than a spongy, wet, fungussy sensation in your socks when doing your morning toilette. The landlady of this establishment was a charmingly witty woman:
Guest: "These eggs are a bit runny this morning."
Landlord: "Not more than I am!"
Ah yes, the rural countryside.

Later on in 2006, Pictoplasma once again invited Jon and Sune to mess up their good name. The annual Pictoplasma Festival in Berlin hosted them this time where they performed a silly talk show on stage, taking turns in being the absurdly interested host and the amusing guest. Jon in particular had the crowd in his hands with his description of what a good salad consisted of. Sune made the crowd go 'ooooooh' when he showed them his corn pipe.

After the talk, Jon and Sune threw a workshop for the good people of Berlin. A gigantic Hello Zuudle map had been created for the event and people were invited to make their own zuudle (a duudle that lives in the zuu) to stick on the map. Gigantic paper rolls were on the floor and hundreds of people crawled and doodled on it and had a jolly good time.

Words: Sune Ehlers, Duudle.dk

Hello Duudle
The first Hello Duudle book was published by Day 14. It was a 170cm long concertina sprawl through a strange duudle world.

Short and silly character bios appeared on the reverse of the pages introducing the reader to their world and nudging them along to invent their own stories for the characters.

Drawing on different papers and textures was an important part of creating the right kind of intimate, tactile feel for the book.

Lost Duudle

1000 hand-drawn paper duudles got separated from the flock one day at Duudleville Avenue during rush hour. They are homeless, hungry and cannot remember their names. Jon and Sune urge you to adopt and look after the enclosed duudle.

Take a picture of it in it's new home, give it a name and tell us what sort of a duudle it is. Email the information to hello@helloduudle.com
Do it now before your duudle runs away!

Name: _____

Duudle Type: _____

Eventually a worldmap of all the adopted duudles will form at www.helloduudle.com
Check in from time to time to see how they're all doing and where they all are.
Thank you for your kind help in looking after this lost duudle.

Please retain this form for future use and in case you forget what you named your duudle.

**Hello Duudle -
The Duudlevile Tales**
Published by Wiggleton Press,
it came in a fancy gold-foiled
box with stickers and a hand
drawn duudle.

1
Hello Duudle Poster
One of two large posters which
were created in a similar way to
the books, with Sune and I emailing
each other images, back and forth.
The posters were produced in an
edition of 1000 each.

2&3
Hello Zuudle Poster
Poster for the Berlin Pictoplasma
conference in 2006. The audience
could create their own doodles
and attach them to the scene.

2

3

Trafalgar Panorama
Mural of Trafalgar in London for the Pizza Express restaurant in Trafalgar, showing a variety of people going about their business, generally unaware of the pink monster looming behind the buildings. The client requested the removal of the dog turd I snuck into the composition incase it put people off their dough balls.

**NOTTINGHAM
CREATIVE NETWORK**
BRINGING CREATIVITY AND
BUSINESS TOGETHER

**THE 2008 SPRING
CONFERENCE SEASON**

1

Berryman

NOTTINGHAM
TRENT UNIVERSITY

prospect *ip*   broadway ⓑ   DE MONTFORT
UNIVERSITY
LEICESTER

WWW.NOTTINGHAMCREATIVE.NET

Design and background illustrations by Casciani Evans Wood
Illustrations by Jon Burgerman

2

3

**NOTTINGHAM
CREATIVE NETWORK**
BRINGING CREATIVITY AND
BUSINESS TOGETHER

**THE 2007 AUTUMN
CONFERENCE SEASON**

4

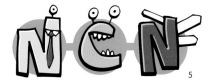

5

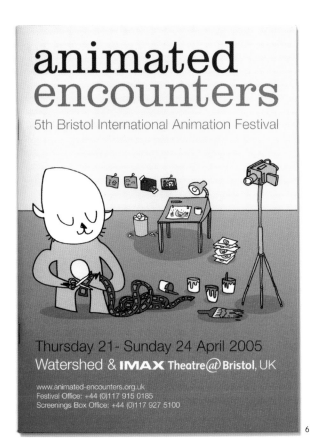

6

7

8

1–5
Nottingham Creative Network
Covers and logo for NCN
conference brochures, design
by Casciani Evans Wood.

6
Animated Encounters
Characters for 'Animated
Encounters' festival.

7
Sick bags
Limited edition sick bags
for Virgin Atlantic.

8
Business Cards
Available from Moo.com

1
Forget-Me-Not
Piece for a charity book to raise money for the Claire Elizabeth Wadley 'Forget-Me-Not' Fund for Leukaemia Research.

2
DGPH
Collaborative poster with Argentinian art collective DGPH.

2

1
NoStore
Poster about bagging up dog mess when out and about with your pet for NoStore.

2
He-Man
A hazy, psychedelic memory of He-Man, Battle Cat, Skeletor, Castle Greyskull and Snake Mountain. I had the toys as a child and remember Skeletor's head was rubbery.

3
Nottingham
Tall doodles of Nottingham, commissioned by Greater Nottingham Partnership. Cloughie is in there, the guy in the bottom right.

1

2

3

Consumption Deficit
A three part nonsense comic.
Commissioned by Stranger
Magazine, UK.

1–5
Propaganda
Flyers for The Propergander
club nights.

6&7
Treeson
Pieces for Bubis' Treeson exhibition.
(He is the white spikey fella)

8
Airside
Print design for the 2008 collection
of Airside's annual t-shirt club.

9
Ice-cream
A paean to ice-cream (hmm pecan
Ice-cream) and warm summers
days, made whilst stuck in a
seemingly endless winter.

6

7

8

9

super powers yeah

1
Super Powers Yeah
Super Powers Yeah follows the misadventures of an ensemble of super heroes endowed with less than super powers. Some of these include having pickling saliva, being able to change TV channels through blinking, cooking frozen pizza with their hands and self inflating until their eyes bulge.

2
Ten 4 Magazine
Characters for Ten 4 Magazine, produced by Ideasfactory.

3
Tattoos
Characters for use as non-permanent tattoos for the book Tattoo Icons published by Victionary.

1

2

3

4

5

6

7

8

1
Juju's Diary
Drawing featured in Juju's 2007 Diary.

2
Baby Sat in His Own Sick
Illustration for Glow Magazine, Canada.

3
Advertising, No Thanks
An exhibition and small magazine produced in Stockholm about the evils of advertising (and curiously produced by man from an ad agency).

4
Don't Panic
Peer Pressure piece for Don't Panic.

5
Rudiger
A little bird (listening to Arab Strap on his ipod) for a charity poster.

6
Jazz Man
Character for New Orleans themed event.

7
The Stinkers
Mini stickers produced by Domestic.fr

8
Mod Biker
Illustration for stuffandnonsense.co.uk

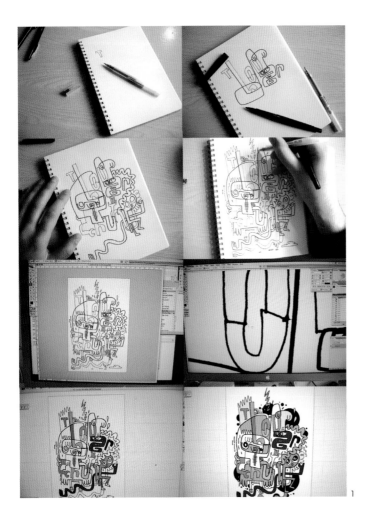

1&2
Thunder Chunky
Piece for a zine by Thunder
Chunky, the photos show the
process of creating it, from
sketchbook to screen.

3–20
Heroes of Burgertown
Doofus (3)
Job: Toy designer.
Significant others:
Troy his pet turtle.

Alfonzo (4)
Achievements: Discovered
a potion for Yetism.
Hobbies: Knitting.

Dinkton Wallis (5)
Awards: World Weevel
Racing Championship.
Punishment: Slapped wrists for
minor race-fixing corruption.

Mendaline (6)
Great at: Hacking into
computer systems.
Bad at: Remembering to
feed her kittens.

Mungton (7)
Insecure about: His height.
Smug about: Movie star status
and best actor award for his
performance in Top Bun.

Collie (8)
Merits: Reigning quiz
show champion.
Demerits: The quiz is called
'The Weakest Stink'.

Piccalilicus (9)
Likes: To groove at the
'Buns and Shakes' club.
Dislikes: Phonies and
their cronies.

Tiny Hero (10)
Best power: Laser vision
can toast bread.
Worse power: Freeze ray
is only lukewarm.

Tiddles Mackenzie (11)
Ambition: To spread love
throughout Burgertown.
Plan to achieve this: Kidnapping
and brainwashing.

The Gobbler (12)
Species: Giant freshwater
river slug snake.
Feeds on: Any children that
happen to fall into his mouth.

Piggbit (13)
Good at: Journalistic exposés.
Bad at: Organisation, lives
in a sty with a string of
disillusioned girlfriends.

Coco Gulab Juman (14)
Famous for: All You Can
Eat competitions.
Infamous for: A temporary
bout of giantism leading to
a city-wide destruction.

Zomboo (15)
Enjoys: Giant turnips.
Enjoyed too much and now must
abstain from: Sherbet dips.

Bimlar Chumlaki (16)
Profession: Artist and player
of the media.
Career highlights: Winning
the Turnip Prize for his work
'The impossibility of sweating in
the mind of the overweight'.

Whilhelm (17)
Band name: Churned Milk.
Best album: Blancmange
on Blancmange.

Yimmi Bites (18)
Occupation: Trainee vampire.
Hobby: Biting people (it's always
nice when your hobby is also
your job).

Tittymon (19)
Smaller than: A panda-dog
Bigger than: A small baby
panda-dog.

Sausage (20)
Dreams of: See another sunrise.
Fears: The chomping jaws of All
You Can Eat champion Coco
Gulab Juman.

Stickers
Various characters made into hand cut (1) and die cut stickers (2). Sold, given away, lost and stuck. See them stuck to stuff on page 297.

1

Symbian Users and Employees
Character designs for internal use at
mobile software company Symbian.

doodles
for
dandies

tees,
apparel
& other
things
you can
show
off with

T-shirt designs, belts, toys
hoodies, sports-wear, and
customised bits and bobs.

Size?

Size? invited me to doodle in their Nottingham store following a tip off from a friend of mine that knew the guys in the shop. A fun afternoon was spent doodling in orange (to match their established colour scheme) fuelled by steaming hot mugs of tea. Woven into the drawing are friends of mine and references to Nottingham. I wonder if anyone has spotted themselves whilst shopping there.

Somebody high up at Size? saw the piece a few weeks later and liked it so much he invited me to collaborate with them on something. Later that year the collection came out featuring a reversible hoody, tee, sweater, belt and umbrella. We had wanted to make socks too but ran out of time. Each item was limited to 300 pieces.

13

14

15

16

T-shirts n stuff
Dadawan (1), Split The Atom (2),
Sideline (3), Owl Movement (4),
Storm (5), I Dress Myself (6),
Imperfect Particles (7), Concrete
Hermit (8&9), The Propergander (10),
Concrete Hermit (11), Concrete (12),
I Dress Myself (13), Sabre (14),
Zoofuku (15), Yes No Maybe (16).

13

14

15

16

17

18

20

19

Some More T-shirts
Jon Burgerman (1), Yoyamart (2),
Ghosticorn (3), Concrete (4),
Sideline (5), 55DSL (6), Imperfect
Particles (7&8), Spunky (9), The Science
Museum (10), Concrete Hermit (11&12),
Candy Culture (13), Funktush (14), The
Science Museum (15), Yes No Maybe (16),
Graniph (17), The Properganger (18), Kid
Robot (19), Funktush (20).

1–7
Love Rabby
Commission to reinvent the
Japanese brand's Love Rabby
rabbit, called Rabby, and her
pals. Various apparel and
instore goodies were produced.

8–9
Burgerland (8), Waistwiggles (9)
Lovely woven belts made in
Switzerland by Yummy Industries.
The white thread on the Burgerland
belt glows in the dark which should
aid taking off your jeans late at night.

8

9

1&3
Adicolor
Hand customised baseball cap
and trainers for Adidas' 'Adicolour'
launch exhibition in Taiwan.

2
Flat Foot Friends
Hand doodled shoes for the
Sneaker Pimp group show
by Lazy Oaf, London.

4
Pinkies
Private commission, traded
for a set of computer themed
plastic coasters.

5–8
Lunar Park
A collection of decals for cars
and other vehicles produced
by Infectious.com, USA.

5

6

7

8

1

2

3

4

5

6

1–9
Concrete Hermit
Page samples from postcard
book 'Sweaty Goolabs'
published by Concrete Hermit.

10–17
Burgertown Stationery
Special stationery items featuring
the Heroes Of Burgertown
characters. Released only
in Taiwan.

7

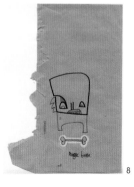

8

9

10

11

12

13

15

17

14

16

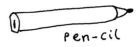

pen-cil

1–8
Nook Art
Merchandise by Australian based
Nook Art, sold worldwide in limited
quantities. The wallet is now
particularly sought after.

Lunchbox (1), 'Doodlesplat' Uni bag
with badge (2), Flat coin purse (3),
'Ellie' pill tin (4), 'Dumbfounded' mini
tin (5), 'Plane' mini tin (6), 'Liars Club'
tri-fold wallet (7), Treasure chest (8).
(Pirates please note - does not
contain any treasure)

9–11
Tote Bags
'Pigbit' heavy canvas tote produced
by Nook Art (9), Light tote bag
produced by Boosey & Hawkes (10),
Tote bag with zip produced by
Flying Cat (11).

12
Sketchel Bags
Devised by Jeremyville, a Sketchel
allows for artworks to be placed in
their front sleeve. The Pink design
was produced as a limited edition,
the others are hand drawn one-offs.

13
Corrupted_Data
USB Memory stick that includes
pre-loaded animations and digital
goodies, produced by Mimoco, USA.

1&2
Doodle Deck
Hand painted skate deck, shown
in progress and completed.

3–5
The Helping Hounds of Hell
Hand painted skate decks for the
charity touring group exhibition
at Helium Cowboy, Hamburg and
Neurotitan, Berlin.

1

2

3

4

5

Canvas 1663

Snowboards
Snowboard produced
by Sims (1), front and
back of boards for Rome
Snowboards (2–9).

1

2

3

4

5

6

7

8

9

RipCurl Summer and Winter Collections '08

RipCurl invited me to collaborate on 'Artist of the Search', Summer Collection. As the collection was to use environmentally friendly materials where possible (organic cotton, recycled materials, soya based surfboards) I invented a character to base the design work around. He's called Greengoon, taking his name from the green credentials of the project and the typically British comedy used in the Goon show. I really like Spike Milligan.

Greengoon is a bit clumsy, often accidentally breaking things (including his arm a few times) but he tries to recycle his cans and paper and leaves beaches, mountains and anywhere else he enjoys his sports neat and tidy. RipCurl liked the artwork for the Summer Collection so much that it was also used for a special Winter Collection too.

ISPO

The ISPO Winter sports show in Munich is where a lot of the pieces I'd made for RipCurl were launched. To celebrate they invited me over to create a mural live at their booth. The visitors to the show then got to colour it in (although some people decided to scrawl rival brands logos over it, tut tut tut).

Burgermenos
The Burgermenos were first created especially for my solo exhibition at Artoyz in Paris. They were hand-painted, on a platform toy called 'Yami' made by Flying Cat. Their name comes from the Tetrameno blocks in the computer game Tetris. Like the blocks in Tetris the Burgermenos try and fit in little nooks and crannies, take on different forms and are sometimes the cause of a lot of frustration.

1

2

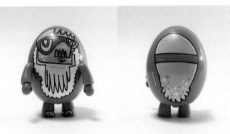

3

4

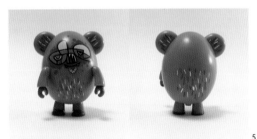

5

6

7

8

9

10

1–14

Burgermenos Egg Qees

These are Burgermenos in the form of 2.5 inch tall Egg Qees. Ears were added to some of the characters in reference to the first iteration of the Burgermenos and to show that they are strange creatures, not strictly egg people. There are twelve characters to collect in total (four of which are mystery figures). There is no point buying just one, you must own them all and complete the set (they get lonely otherwise).

Tootles (1), Jitter (2), Bubba (3), Snowbert (4), Grimock (5), Zambo (6), Jonquil (7), Hambo (8), Bambo (9), Hemple (10), Lolly (11), Bazoonoo (12).

Produced by Toy2r, Hong Kong, as part of the 'Magic of Color' series 4.

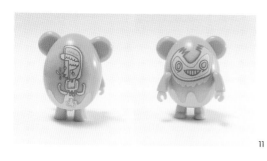

11

12

13

14

pantone 212
pantone 196
pantone 278
pantone black
White

Mfamwe

hair raised and sits over the head
slightly raised hair detail
lounge painted inside mouth
printed cheek make up
grooved zip details
indented holes on the belt
raised belt and belt buckle
hand to grip newspaper
boots wider than legs
slightly raised hair detail
printed cheek make up
raised pocket detail
thumb

Sydney Morning Herald
Development of characters for
the Australian newspaper, The
Sydney Morning Herald. Starting
from rough concept drawings,
the characters were honed and
tweaked over several drafts,
responding to client feedback, until
turnaround drawings were made.

The turnarounds act as guides
for both the computer generated
3D models of the gang and the
hand sculpted figurines. The toys
only appeared in Australia as
promotion for the newspaper.
I still have a stash of them under
my bed and will listen to any offers
for them before covertly putting
them on eBay.

1

2

4

5

1–6
Qee
Hand painted Qees for various Toy2r exhibitions. Produced by Toy2r, Hong Kong.

7&8
ODM Watch
Motion sensor watch with a silicon strap which feels really nice and soft. Produced by ODM, Singapore.

9
We Speak Football Trexi
Limited edition Trexi for Coca-Cola for the 2006 World Cup. Produced by Play Imaginative, Singapore.

10–12
Trexi
Hand painted Trexi (10) used as a guide to make the red Trexi (11&12). This was a secret 'chase' figure for the second series of the collectable toys. Produced by Play Imaginative, Singapore.

10

11

12

1

2

3

1–3
Fatty Boom-Boom
Fatty Boom-Boom has a very sweet tooth that sometimes leads him to having an upset stomach. The 2.5 inch toy is part of the fourth series of the Dunny collectables. Original drawings of Fatty Boom-Boom (4) were given away to those attending the many launch parties held for the series in America. Produced by Kid Robot, USA.

4
Tea-Bear
Tea-Bear was found roaming the lush, green hills of Derbyshire before being forced into the life of an English butler by his unruly master Dr. Doodlebaum. Nobody knows that Tea-Bear has been secretly weeing into the brew and putting tiny bear plops in the scones. Whatever you do don't ask for a frothy coffee.

Tea-Bear is part of a collection of 8 inch Dunnys along with bears by ILoveDust and Tado, produced by Kid Robot, USA. The collective is called 3 Bears. Some information about 3bears might be found at we3bears.com

 Salty black honey

 Tea cup and saucer

 Half eaten scone

 Handle of cup to fit in Dunnys hand

 Jam viewable through bite

All raisins in scone slightly raised

Saucer to be separate from cup

4

1–4

Pen Tent

Sharpie sent me lots of pens. This is kind I thought, I like pens. Then they sent me a big white tent and some flags. The motive behind their initial generosity suddenly became apparent. The tent got to go to the Glastonbury Festival, whilst I had to make do and watch it on TV. Still, it rained all weekend so perhaps it was for the best.

5

Action Man

Customised Action Man for the '40-40' event, celebrating 40 years of the toy. I had one as a child and it had fuzzy hair and moveable eyes.

I called the customisation 'Skin Burns Action Man' but after he was photographed in a suggestive pose, the press thought the theme was something else entirely. It was even discussed on the BBC breakfast programme on TV. It must have been a slow news day.

DIG DIG

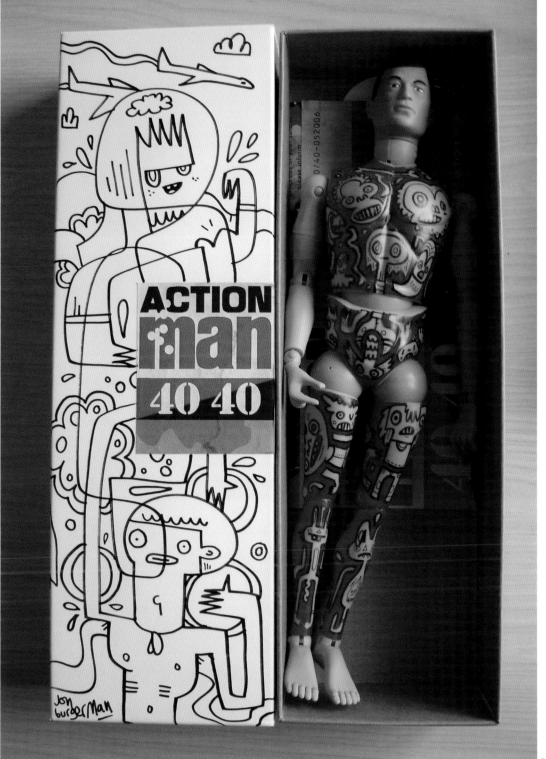

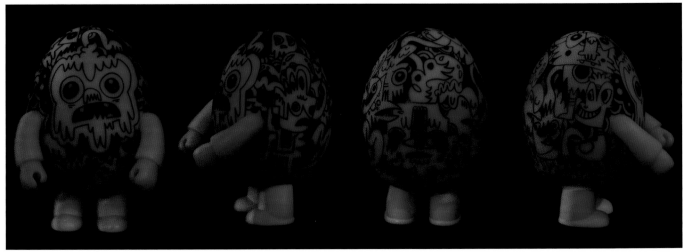

8

9

4

5

6

7

1–3
Egg Qees
Various hand painted 8 inch
Egg Qees, including a glow in
the dark (2) model. Toy produced
by Toy2r, Hong Kong.

4–7
Fat Cap
Customised Fat Cap, 20 inch toy
for charity auction 'The Paint Ball' in
New York. Event and toy produced
by Kid Robot, US.

8&9
Munny
Hand doodled Munny for private
commissions (Aaron used his
customised Munny to propose
to Julie, who said yes).

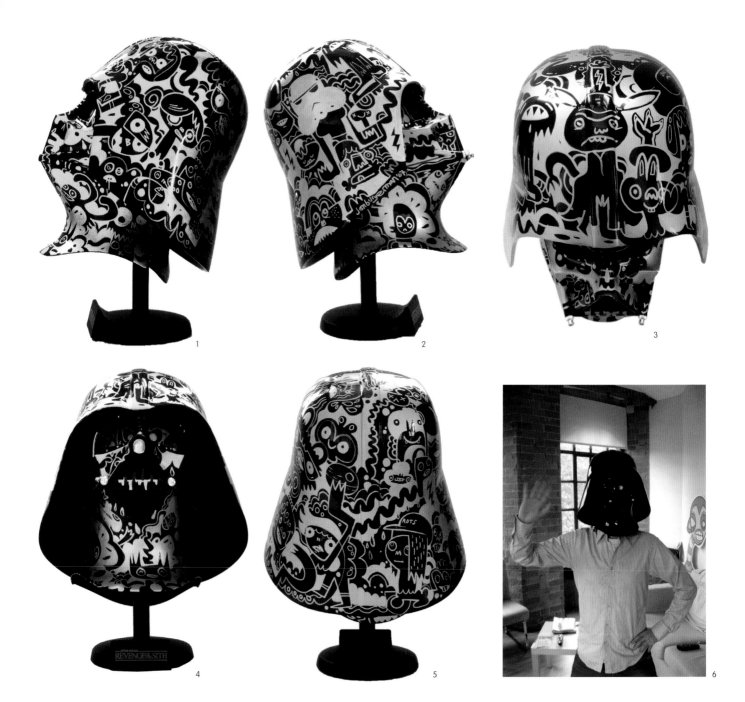

1
2
3
4
5
6

**1–6
Vader Project**
Hand customised Darth Vader helmet,
with a silver pen, for the giant Star Wars
Celebration exhibition at Excel, London.
Wearing the helmet made me breathe a
lot deeper and heavier than usual...

Note - Darth would have looked really good in a
pink shirt, enough with dressing in black all time.

**7&8
Design Skins**
Vinyl design skins for various electronic
gadgets including iPods, laptops, mobile
phones and handheld gaming consoles.
Nintendo DS version shown. Produced by
Dein-Design.com

7

8

1

2

3

4

5

6

7

8

9

10

11

1&2
Slip Mats
Fuzzy slipmats to place underneath all your beloved Van Halen LPs, produced by Rootdesign.

3
Mustard Disc
Design for the UK team Mustard, showing an Ultimate Frisbee player energetically 'laying out'. When I enjoy 'laying out' it is normally on the sofa.

4–7
Zeebzeebs
The Zeebzeebs are cheeky characters who live underground and make street art late at night. They hope one day Hollywood actors will collect their work. They have reappeared across many different projects including record sleeves, stickers, animations, comics and plush toys.

8–10
Mouse Qee
Hand painted Mouse Qee for a private commission. Toy produced by Toy2r, Hong Kong.

11
Circus Punk
Hand customised Circus Punk called Pinky McFluff, blank model produced by Circus Punks, USA.

12
Circus Punk
Limited edition Circus Punk called The Clown King Fluffer, produced by Circus Punks, USA.

12

2

3

1
Bart Simpson Qee
Hand painted Bart Simpson Qee for
various exhibitions organised and
produced by Toy2r, Hong Kong.

2–4
Remixed Record
Painted 76rpm record for an
exhibition in Phonica Records,
London. Royal Mail kindly
contributed to the piece by
delivering it in several pieces.
The exhibition was curated by
Wear It With Pride.

JON BURGERMAN

JON BURGERMAN
WWW.JONBURGERMAN.COM

WIWP and Jon Burgerman would like to thank the Royal Mail for kindly participating in the
Remixed Exhibition. Not only did they do a starling job of delivering it to WIWP HQ but they also
got into the spirit of the exhibition. Not satisfied with the complete, non segmented format that
everyone else had adopted, they decided to take the Remix concept a step further by presenting
it in pieces! Thank you Royal Mail and your clumsy, butter fingers!

4

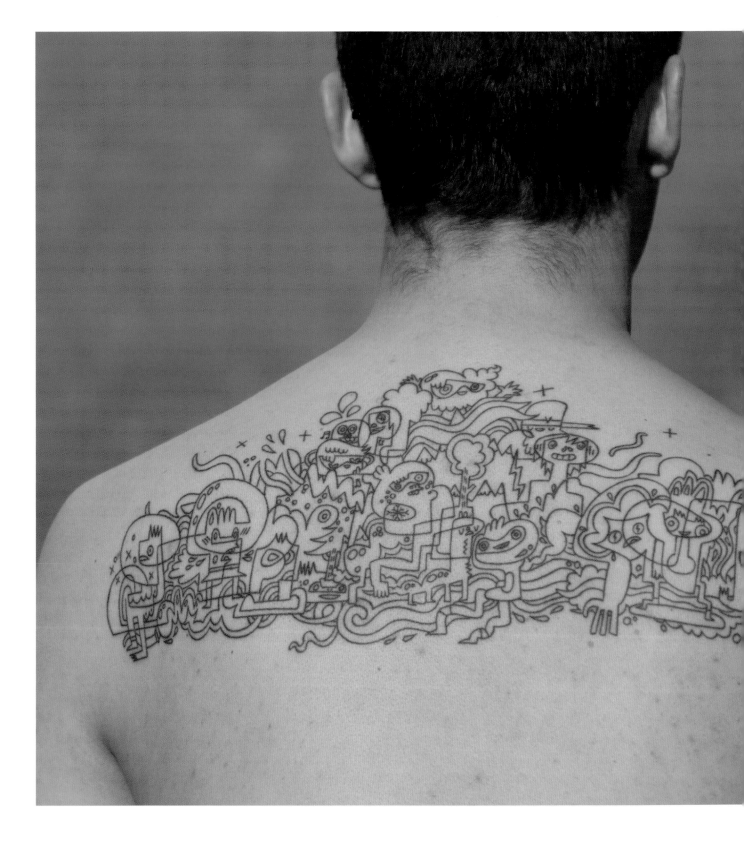

Pablo's Tattoo
Pablo wanted a big tattoo on his back
so I created this especially for him,
featuring some of his loves in life.

In return he sent me a CD of music
from Chile and a wooden 'Mapuche'
toy with a pop-up winkle.

1–4
Thunder Egg
Doodled walls for
Thunder Egg, Manchester.

1

3

4

Sixty Showroom, Netherlands
A tower of bumblebee doodles
reaching the skies

I was invited by the Sixty Group (Miss Sixty) to paint a mural in their fancy head office and showroom in Amsterdam.

I started by doodling as quickly as possible on the massive wall, until it was all dark outside. Then the painting commenced, which took about three times longer than the doodling did. I had to return to Amsterdam a second time to finish the whole wall.

Scaffolding had to be constructed because the cherry picker could not extend high enough. I also brought my friend Dave with me to help with the painting on my second visit but he spent most of his time eating the biscuits found in the coffee bar on the second floor. Admittedly they were very nice biscuits.

1–3
Hot Wheels
Customised Hot Wheels VW Van by Stu Witter and myself for a forty artist group show curated by Gallery 1988, Los Angeles. We travelled across America, coast to coast, in this baby (after shrinking ourselves down of course) a few decades ago on an amazing trip. It was somewhere around Barstow when we first started to see the bats...

4&5
Own Your C
Own Your C is a charity in Colorado, helping explain the facts about smoking to children. The converted ice-cream van travels around handing out free lollys and information. Details can be found at Ownyourc.com

1

2

3

4

5

Hotel 60, Italy
Boutique hotel with a site specific medley of incessant doodlescrawling over its walls

Hotel 60 is the first hotel project by the Miss Sixty Group. It is located in Riccione on the East coast of Italy, which is a popular holiday destination for young Italian hipsters. I travelled to Bologna from London by plane and then caught a train out to the coast. On the train I ate some sandwiches I had prepared the previous day as rural Italy zipped by.

European artists were commissioned to create new works on site in various rooms (I was the sole representative from the UK to be asked to do a room). The photos show the room in an unfinished state (note - the health and safety defying hanging wires and loose plug sockets). The hotel opened on 19th June 2006, with all the furniture and fittings installed, some of which partially blocked my work.

For the installation I wanted to create a wallpapering of drawings, doodles and scrawls to crawl over the walls, sockets, air conditioning vents and even the ceiling. It would be an overload of communication, a response to the frustrations I experienced whilst there due to my inability to successfully communicate to anyone in Italian.

It was a challenge to generate such a vast number of drawings in a short space of time (two days). My brain cut out after a couple of hours on the first morning, leaving my hand to continue drawing in a frenzied motion. This led to interesting and unexpected results for my work, and captured the essence of what I believe doodling to involve; the lapse in premeditated thought and action. As the hours rolled past and the natural light faded my drawings became looser and more gestural.

The heat swelled and the dusty hotel, now void of its Elton John crooning workmen, took on an ominous presence. The half finished building site on the edge of an empty holiday resort, bathed in evening violets and blues felt quite forsaken. This further influenced my drawings, making them intense in their density. When viewed as broken down elements each doodle could be taken as playful, when amassed as a total they gave the room a menace, like deranged scratches on an asylum cell wall.

Half way into the second day I decided to stop drawing, I was working on the lower ceiling at the time. The mdf dust showering out from the jigsaw in the nearby corridor had begun to make my face smart with allergies. My eyes were blurred and red. I took a walk along the beach and saw a small lizard crossing the road. Later that evening I ate some pasta at the hotel I was staying at and struggled to explain to the non-English speaking manager I needed to leave early the next day. She mimed unlocking the front door and slipping the key back through the letter box, which I mimicked for real the following morning upon my departure.

DreamBagsJaguarShoes
Large mural in Dreambagsjaguarshoes,
London, exhibited with felt pen artwork (left)
for a group show organised by Darren Firth
of Wear It With Pride.

warm wine & anxiety
art works & exhibit-ions

Exhibitions where I've drawn all over the walls etc, plus more traditional exhibitions, group shows, personal art projects, paintings, drawings.

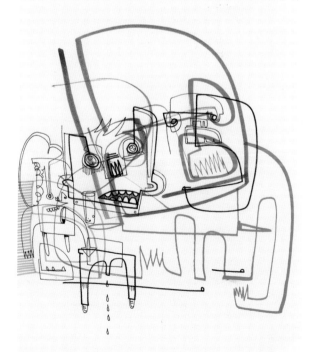

2 Steps Back
Drawings for a touring exhibition asking designers and artists who use a computer in their work to take some steps back (I guess two) and generate works just using pens on paper. Curated by 55DSL.

On the Wall
Concrete, Amsterdam
May 5 – June 16, 2007

Presented by TAG and Concrete in Amsterdam, On The Wall was a show of improvised drawings that bled beyond the hung panels onto the surrounding surfaces. No planning, compositions or roughs were taken into the space to work from. The challenge with this and the other large scale improvised pieces I've made is to keep drawing even when you feel you cannot think of anything else to draw.

Strange and brilliant things can be found in the deep, barrel-pit of your mind, if you tunnel down far enough. If you are working like this for an extended period of time you can enter the doodle-zone, where you are neither thinking about what you are drawing or thinking about what you could possibly draw; your mind, hand and pen become one and you are swept along on inky, roller-coaster lines in an almost transcendental state.

1

2

3

4

1–4

Angel Row Gallery, Window: 06

An over-blown and over-saturated explosion of celebration and whimper. A salute to my time spent in Nottingham, from wide-eyed student optimism to tired irreverence, taking in pigeons and soggy, soiled parks, estranged locals and arts and crafts along the way.

5–7

Napkin Exhibition

Biro doodles on paper napkins for an exhibition in Soho, London. Curated by Jacki Lang, the funds raised from the show went to food aid charities.

5

6

7

Free Lunch
Analogue Books, Edinburgh
March 15 – April 14, 2007

Free Lunch was an exhibition of doodles, prints, paintings and drawings shown at Analogue Books. Amongst strange characters and colourful artworks the notion of getting something for nothing and the expectation that this brings was explored. Visitors to the private view were encouraged to bring small lunch items with them in exchange for an unspecified gift.

Some brought home-made pies and manwiches (giant sandwiches) whilst others copped out and just came with a left over chocolate bar from their lunch. All were rewarded with a small, signed, limited edition Gocco print and I got several bags of swag to munch through on my long train journey home the next day.

power Lunch

Magical Flakes

we are the egg-heads.

my friends are idiots

all gone - gones

It's nearly time!

the healing hands of salad

Free Lunch drawings
and doodles.

Free Lunch paintings
Praying Characters
and Google Eyes.

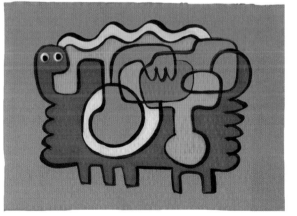

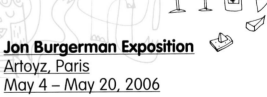

Jon Burgerman Exposition
Artoyz, Paris
May 4 – May 20, 2006

Down in the dungeons of Artoyz, Paris, lies their art gallery which I furnished with prints, drawings, canvases, hand painted toys and other bits and bobs. Next door to Artoyz is a wonderful wine and cheese shop.

After the exhibition opening we were invited over to look at their cellar and to sample some of the delights to be found within, which were magnifique!

this food is alive

Artoyz Print
Yellow Drunk.

Artoyz Prints
Red Sun and Wolf Man.

Hypercolourphagia
ROJO® Artspace Barcelona
November 8 – December 1, 2007

A collection of super saturated, frenzied, stretched canvas prints. The works teeter dangerously along the point of palatable joyfulness and sickly overload, pondering notions of consumption and the follies associated with over indulgence.

The pieces (including Koolaid opposite) were created with multiple hand drawn works being broken apart and deftly reassembled digitally, keeping a sketchbook scrawl rawness tempered with a sugar encrusted palette.

Hypercolourphagia Prints
This spread Darkwheat and
previous spread Bottled Water
and Burnt Tongue.

Hypercolourphagia Prints
This spread Wheat,
next spread Pinch and
Toothpaste For Dinner.

Hypercolourphagia Prints
This spread Peas Please
and Peanut, next spread
Reheat and Pique.

Immature Miniatures
Mad Turnip, Paris
April 14 - May 31, 2007

A collaborative exhibition extravaganza with the cheeky UK based design duo Tado. Each piece in the show was worked on by myself and Tado, including canvases, drawings, t-shirts and toys. The canvases were created by taking one of my warped landscape drawings and slowly adding colour and characters to them. Each piece was given a distinct colour way to help define its mood. Whilst these were worked on via email the drawings were made during a day spent together in Sheffield. I was treated to a baked potato whilst there and a visit to a much talked about Chinese bun shop, both were excellent. The toys were hand cast and then drawn on and the plush toys were printed each side with a special heat sealed transfer and then sewn together by the tireless fingers of Marion 'Maz' Hawkes. The title of the show probably reflects on us as much as it refers to the characters featured in the artworks.

Immature Miniatures Prints
Previous spread Unfathomable
Jamboree, this spread Grizzle
Treats and Avocado Lush.

Immature Miniatures Prints
This spread Poppy Putrescent,
Wisdom of Gewgaw, preliminary
drawings and characters. Next
spread collaborative pen drawings.

1

2

3

1
Lazy Oaf
Canvas prints for a mini exhibition
at the London store.

2
Super Heroes
Limited edition canvas print for the
big group exhibition 'Under The
Influence: A Tribute to Stan Lee'
at Gallery 1988, Los Angeles.

3
PaperCuts
Laser cut paper piece for the
group show at Dreambags-
jaguarshoes, London.

4&5
Rash Works
Posca pen drawings on paper
for the group exhibition 'Den
of Iniquity' at The Rogues'
Gallery, Belfast.

4

5

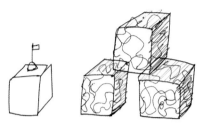

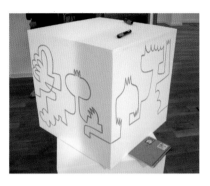

The Elements of
Colourful Surroundings
Novas Gallery, London
August 2 – September 8, 2006

United by illustration as one of their languages of visual communication, the participating artists in this group show exhibited new pieces that had been specially created in response to the gallery space. The exhibition burst full of surreal, expressive and psychedelic images that contained irony, sarcasm and humour, offering the viewer a different way to see the surroundings and its inhabitants.

I drew on some big cubes. I had the idea of stacking them up and placing a flag on the top. The gallery was very posh and clean (not something I was used to) so I thought I would create my own personal white cubes, and then I would feel comfortable enough to freely deface them.

The exhibition was curated by Liga Kitchen.

1
Pink Turnip
Collaboration with Stu Witter.
For the show 'Toy Saves Children'
in Singapore curated by FURI FURI.

2
Pun Band Guitar
Customised guitar for the group
exhibition 'Sounds Like Another
Custom Show' in New York,
curated by Syrup Kids.

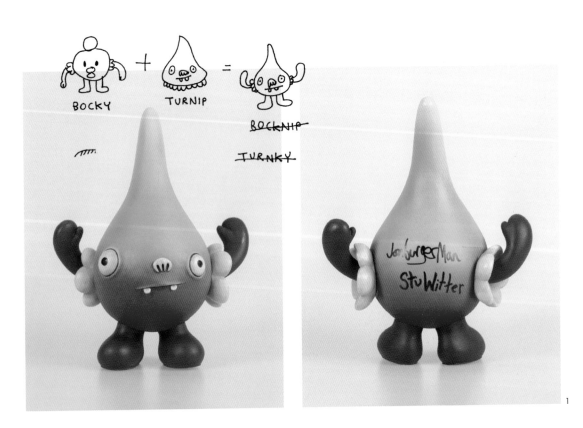

BOCKY + TURNIP = BOCKNIP

TURNKY

2

1

2

3

4

1–7

Paintings

Jawbreaker, Posca pen on cardboard (1).
Around and around, Posca pen on pizza stained cardboard (2).
Kids In The Park Not Doing Much, Posca pen on cardboard (3).

Crawling Insects, acrylic paint and Posca pen on cardboard (4).
Whole Inside, acrylic paint and Posca pen on cardboard (5).
Snooze, acrylic and elusion paint with Posca pen on cardboard (6).
Sounds You Hear Whilst Asleep, acrylic and elusion paint with Posca pen on cardboard (7).

5

6

7

Drawings on Old Cereal Boxes
(Generally high fibre cereals)
Reduce, reuse, recycle, and
that goes for your art ideas
and materials too. These pieces
were exhibited at Teaforest,
Culver City, California.

New Voices
Felt pen, biro and pencil drawings
for the 4Wall launch group show
'New Voices' at The Menier
Chocolate Factory, London.

Mini (1), Nineteen Something or
Other (2), Chump & Chumpette (3).

CHUMP

POTATO

UP

your....

3

1

2

3

4

5

6

7

8

4

1–5
Tangerine Scream
Collection of Posca pen drawings on paper along the theme of good things going rotten.

6–9
Bag It Up
Drawings on brown paper bags for a group show at Madame Edgar, Canada. The bags were auctioned on eBay, no idea what happened to the proceeds...

1

2

3

4

5

1–5
2000 AD Show
Re-imagining (doodle-mangling)
of popular 2000AD characters for
'ZarJaz' group show in London.

6–9
Paintings on card
For 'Pop Invaderz' group show
at MondoPOP, Rome, Italy.

6

7

8

9

1

2

3

4

5

6

7

8

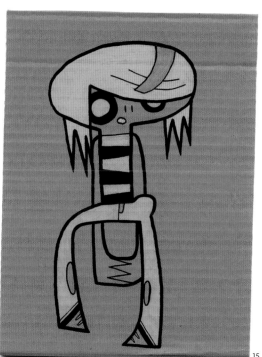

1–8
Various Works on Card
Paintings and Posca pen drawings on card. These pieces and others like them have popped up in smaller exhibitions I've been involved in over the last few years.

9–15
Card Girls
Collection of paintings of girls, made for an online exhibition on an old version of my website.

Drawing is a Verb.
Drawing is a Noun.
Stone Gallery, Dublin
September 28 -
October 17, 2006

A group show in Ireland exploring drawing as both an activity and an object. The busyness of the pieces over emphasises the gestural actions made to generate the drawings.

Card Works
Posca, pens and
biro on card.

Upper Space
A2 sized drawings, Posca pen on paper, for the launch show 'This Is Us' at Upper Space, Manchester.

ROJO® Out
International Outdoor Urban Art
Exhibition, featured 15 selected
artists, asked to create specific
artworks to be shown on 43
giant billboards across streets of
Barcelona's metropolitan area.

Duhprishus
ROJO® artspace Milano
March 13 - April 11, 2008

Subject to impulsive, unpredictable lines and cascades of pop colour, Duhprishus licks the whimwham flutterbyes straight out of your eyes and smears them right back on to the walls. This full force installation with un-twistable stomachs and detachable parts, was created during an intense period of work over the course of three days on site in the gallery space.

It was intended that both of the opposing large panels function as works within their own right, with the smaller panels contained being able to also exist on their own terms. This was the debut show in the new ROJO® art space in Milan. The opening also saw the launch of my monograph book Gribba Grub, published by ROJO®. Special thanks to Dr Lorenzo Gatti for his tireless work in helping realise the exhibition.

Mild Violence
Large canvas painted live
for a Boosey & Hawkes
showcase in London.

1

2

3

1–3
Paintings
Acrylic paint and
Posca pen on canvas.

4–7
Candy Dublin
Paintings made live, alongside
artist Chris Judge, at a bar in
Dublin (where they plied me with
drinks so shamefully I cannot
remember the name of the
bar). The bar staff were juggling
bottles and glasses as they made
drinks which sort of eclipsed
the spectacle of paint drying.
Afterwards we had to run away
with our paintings too. It was an
odd night.

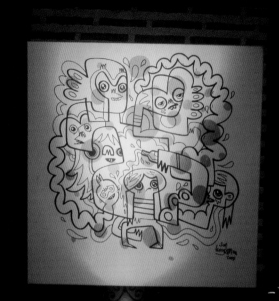

4

5

6

7

The Colour Room
Space4 Gallery, Peterborough
August 5 – October 29, 2006

Doodling in Peterborough with Sune
Ehlers to create a walk through
colouring-in room, to accompany
the last showing of Pictoplasma's
'Characters At War' group exhibition.
See page 64 for more information
on Hello Duudle and Pictoplasma.

The Colour Room,
being coloured in.

Quadcity
Derby City Centre
May – September, 2007

I was commissioned by QUAD in Derby to create a large scale mural outside in the city centre, Market Place, on the hoardings of the construction site of the new QUAD building (set to open summer 2008). As well as commissioning a new piece of work QUAD hoped it would draw attention to their new building and stir public interest. The commission requested that while I would be creating all the work, the public should be able to contribute in some way.

Together with QUAD I devised a questionnaire which was handed out in the streets and sent to schools in the region. It featured a series of questions (what is your favourite colour, if Derby was a food what would it be and why... etc) and space for people to fill in a self-portrait. Four thousand of these were sent back to QUAD and the responses formed the basis for the mural.

I referenced various things from the questionnaires in the mural, whilst interweaving in various Derby landmarks. Other drawings were added to these following incidents and conversations I experienced during the four days outside drawing. Lots of people came and spoke to me as I worked on the piece, happy to idly chat, suggest ideas, point out various mistakes I had made and let me know where I could get a good cob (sandwich) from.

Once the drawing was complete I photographed it and generated a simple colour guide. Members of the public were invited, for a period of four days, to come and colour in the piece. A wide range of people from around Derby attended, and a few people, who had filled in the questionnaire or had spoken to me the previous week, even recognised themselves in the mural.

Day One
A little amount of doodling was done, in amongst the frequent rain showers. A lot of people stopped by to see what I was doing and have a chat. Distraction also came from the local newspaper sending a reporter and then photographer. BBC Radio Derby also sent a guy to interview me and record some spots to play through-out the week. We listened to the report on the radio later that afternoon and, as I suspected, I sounded silly.

Day Two
There was a period of heavy rain, the fragile garden gazebo that had been erected to offer cover from any rain proved quite ineffectual. Fliers and brochures got wet and the Poundland biscuits got soggy. Some doodling was done later on in the day once the sun made a late appearance.

Day Three
The sun shone, I got burnt and I nearly finished the long panel.

Day Four
A nice relaxing Saturday in Derby Market Place. The panels were all done and I had a great vegan lasagna for my lunch. The colouring in began a week after the drawing had been completed.

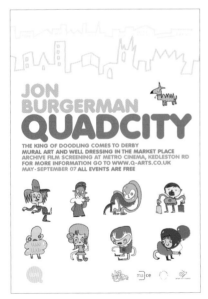

Colour Me In
Young Creative Network
at the Royal College of Art
August 31 - September 3, 2007

Colour Me In wall, done in a day,
for a group show curated by
Young Creative Network at the
Royal College of Art, London. There
were lots of smart, young, sexy,
creative people at the exhibition
opening. It was quite intimidating.

1

3

2

4

5

6

7

1–5
Colour Me Butter
In conjunction with the Singapore Design Festival 2007, the Butter Factory presented live doodling with 'Colour Me Butter'. The public were invited to submit their photos to the Butter Factory to be possibly included in the muraloodle.

Upon completion of the mural visitors to the space could colour it in, any way they liked. Some kept within the lines and others went all crazy and strayed outside of the lines. A lot of the drawings in the mural reference my experience of visiting Singapore for the first time.

6&7
Big Draw
Window drawing at the Turnpike Gallery, Leigh.

Designersblock: Illustrate
September 15 – 23, 2007

A huge colouring in room housed
in an empty retail unit as part of the
eighty artists group show spread over
a four acre site in Islington, London.

scribbles in sketch- books

A look inside my sketchbooks where the limits of my doodles are the limits of my world. Also includes envelope noodling and little comics.

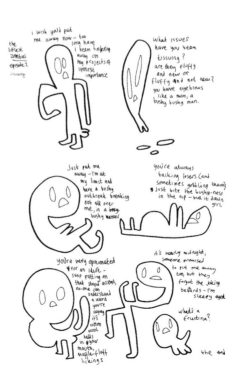

trippy froggy

bad bad bad

tired little
legs. cha
cha cha

BRIN
WASH

Dad
Dance

DOLPHINPLANT

FRUIT
LITTLE
CLUB

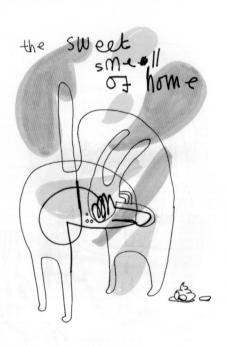

the sweet
smell
of home

sweaty
hills

FRƎWSH

cobbler

8 Monday

Starburst fruit chew, found on street corner. [unopened]

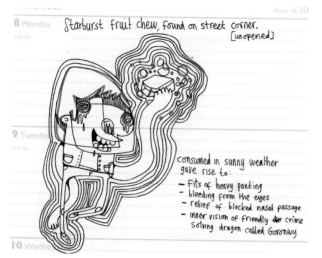

9 Tuesday

consumed in sunny weather gave rise to:
- Fits of heavy panting
- bleeding from the eyes
- relief of blocked nasal passage
- inner vision of friendly crime solving dragon called Goronwy

10 Wednes

PLEDGE

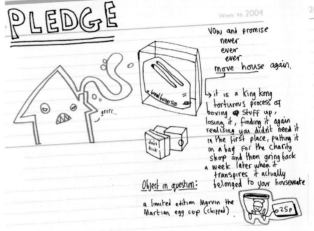

VOW and promise
never
ever
ever
move house again.

grrrr...

→ it is a king kong torturous process of boxing up stuff up, losing it, finding it again realising you didn't need it in the first place, putting it in a bag for the charity shop and then going back a week later when it transpires it actually belonged to your housemate

Object in question:

a limited edition Marvin the Martian egg cup (chipped)

25p

Confession/question

Sunday 28

After love making (the rare + sacred act between two consenting adults — one slightly inebriated on cheap white wine from the 24 hour garage, the other thankful as hell)
Is it wrong to be thinking of checking your emails?

Notes

"call now"

"calls charged at extortimate rate to help fund reality tv shows + sweat shops in Burma

November
M T W T F S S
1 2 3 4 5 6 7
8 9 10 11 12 13 14
15 16 17 18 19 20 21
22 23 24 25 26 27 28
29 30

The bathroom Floor

wasn't carpeted when we moved in — it just hasn't ever been cleaned
the horror of...

Natural Matting (soft + wirey at the same time)

* Should anything touch floor it is immediately removed and destroyed in a controlled enviroment.

clean cotton buds
An unhealthy build up of ear gunk has become a problem since the cotton buds hit the deck.

Resolution: clean or pay someone to come in (note: could ask mum)

There is Life on Mars

FACT: (this was read in a book)

Tiny germs (everywhere)

they are the size of full stops.

ZOOM
WOOZ

a full stop (which is tiny)

TIME TO PANIC

The Martians will take over the Earth, posing as Punctuation. Slowly but surely, they will re-punctuate our greatest literary works thus making them completely incomprehensible. We will all become more and more stupid over time- therefore more likely to lose the Martians challenge of an essay writing contest "who should rule the Earth, discuss."

A+

smug glow

HUH

?

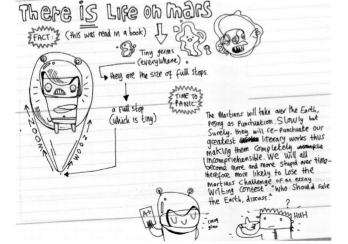

Constant thudding

and soft mutterings at 3am

→ Next door neighbours are young student types, with their outlandish hair + large trousers

z z z

WIKID

RAD DUDE!

Let's drink and party and then set off a smoke alarm

Strange smells seep from their windows — invading precious clean air space.

egg fish bad

Retreat → under dining room table - listen but try not to listen... can clearly hear laughter + fun through the walls. must phone police

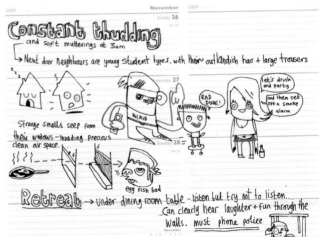

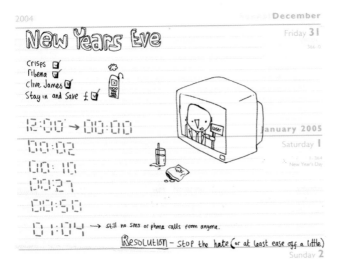

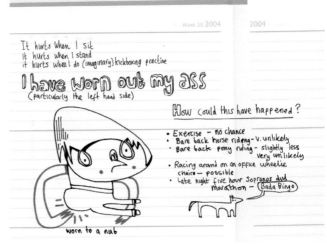

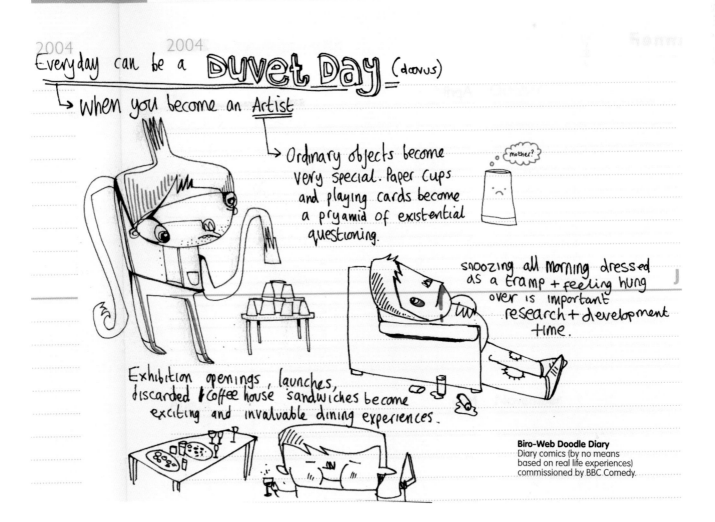

Biro-Web Doodle Diary
Diary comics (by no means
based on real life experiences)
commissioned by BBC Comedy.

SUPER LUNGS

don't make me lamp you son.

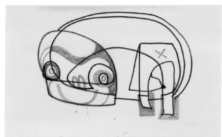

Pak choi

you are not my hero.

Crappy dreams

glen close

BAD FEELINGS

SELFISH SUPPER MAKER

brown trousers

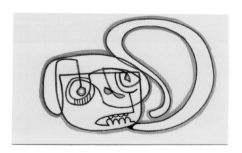

CRISPS FOR DINNER

small brain

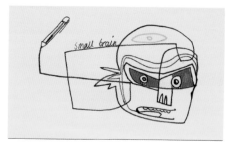

greatest hit

NOT CLOSE

I maybe the biggest cock in the world but I have the smallest willy.

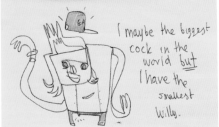

baked Beans

your dignity is a far far away

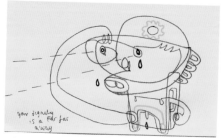

Stubby

DUNST

t.l.e.

1&2
Doodles with Gary Baseman, who I sat next to during a lecture at the Pictoplasma festival, Berlin, 2006

shops

Walking

woman

english teeth.

Walking #2

Rodney Alan Greenblat

$ Coney Island

NY

gone fishin'

\#\#People

chad is charles
in american

yo chad.

Food
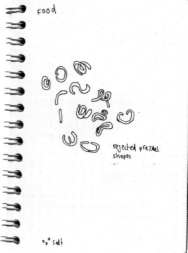

rejected prezdel
shapes

"o" salt

Subway

sleeping

Breakfast

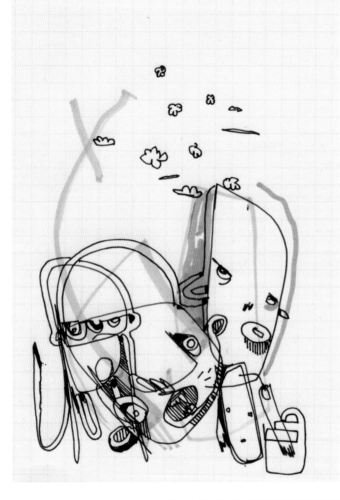

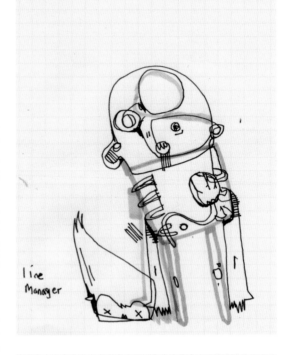

line Manager

Management process

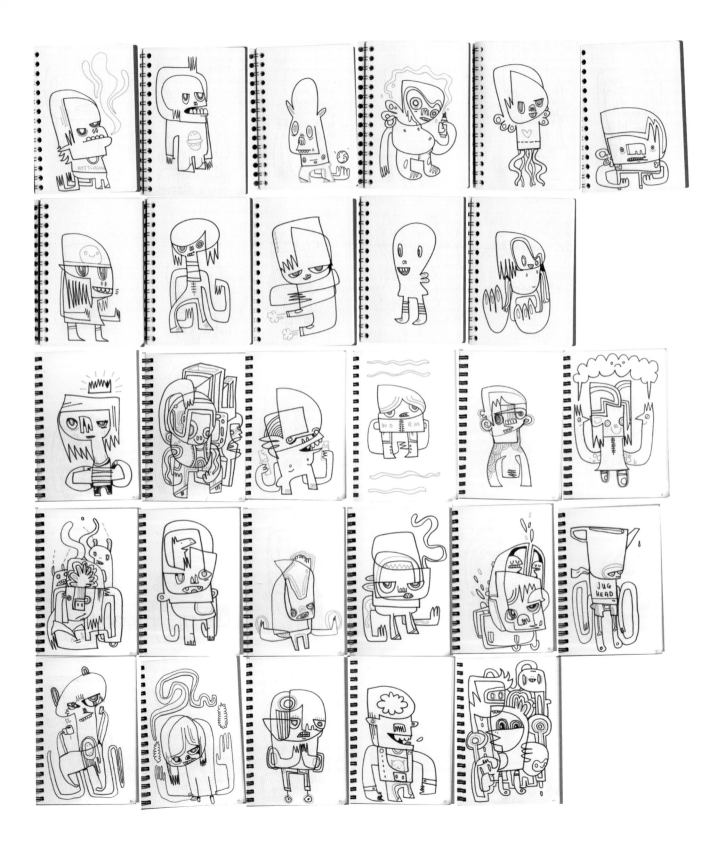

Jmbuyerman

Leather Face

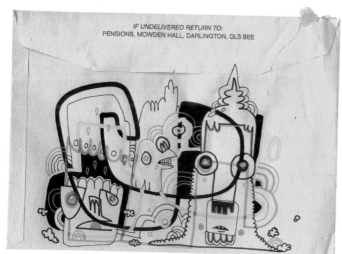

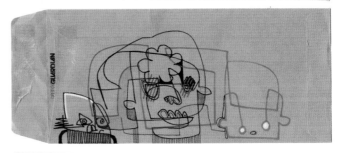

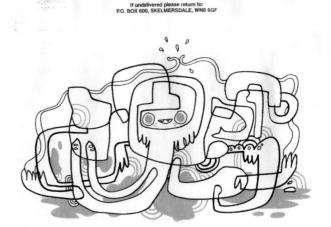

Jonburgerman

EOP39

PRIVATE

SF 1703

FOOME
FRUPTUS

under
the rug
collab-
orations,
curios &
oddities

Odd work with odd people
and other things we didn't
know where-else to put.

Badges
Assorted badges for Pin Pops,
Alive, Instant Life Show, Nookart,
Stereohype, I Love Cooking,
Immature Miniatures, Science
Museum and Nottingham
Creative Network.

WipEout Pure Artist Track
A slow cruise through the Burgertown Races

SONY invited me to design a level for WipEout Pure on the Playstation Portable. The level, along with three other artists tracks were available as a free download from SONY, once you had purchased the game. I was presented with a blank track to work with and given no other brief or direction. I was free to design everything that would fit around, over and under the racing track.

Whilst enjoying computer games I am also rubbish at them so I decided I wanted to make my track one where you did not have to zoom around it as quickly as possible. I wanted it to be enjoyable to cruise along it at your own pace, taking in the sights and characters along the way.

Overall I hoped the track would be a drive through piece of work. The 3D model making and all technical stuff was skilfully handled by the brainiacs at SONY Liverpool, though they did let me make the squeaky sound effects for the jumping sausages.

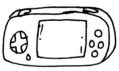

Sausage + mix and match expressions

Coco Gulab Juman

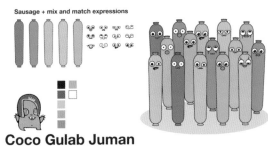

Eyes are rounded and do not come out further than the helmet rim

Rim of helmet pertudes slightly

Helmet fits over head

Nostrils indented slightly

Little ripples of fat folding from the helmet

Fork

Faint suggestion of a bottom

— halo

Burgertown

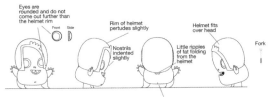

Beam comes out from the robots mouth and is shot into a mirroed robot on the other side of the track.

Light revolves round like a police car light and it glows

Eye could blink every so often

Robot head comes out from track wall

Laser beam come out from mouth pipe.

The light of the beam is dotted and glows

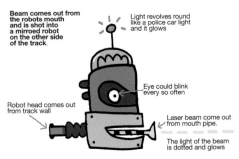

these 'bolts' coming out from the mass of characters. maybe as triggered events.

these could be flat with some reliefs and the bubbles could be rounded.

blinking eyes?

Holding a cup which the ship drives into. Half of the hands are painted onto the track.

ship

The WEEVEL DOME

ALL HAIL
KING WEEVEL

!ALERT!
GHOST WEEVELS

FEAR THE WAY OF THE WEEVEL

ANIMALS CAN LICK AS WELL AS BITE

Dinkton Wallis, Weevel Racer

Mini Lanks, Minimum wage banner holders

Hello Card Girl, Giant greeting statue

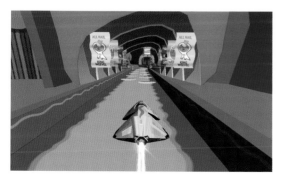

<u>Worryknott</u>

Worryknott is a collaborative work between myself and artist Stuart Witter, of UK based makers Collective Lowlife. Worryknott is not a toy, it is a desktop sculpture. You can curate your own table top exhibition and invite small pets like mice and hamsters to visit your newly made gallery space.

The piece charts the inevitability of getting tangled up in anxiety and its ultimate choking futility. This was the first time I had tried to realise a mass of doodles in a 3D form. Each hand cast white resin sculpture, 135 x 120 x 80mm, comes hand numbered and signed. It is finished in a protective lacquer, comes with a nice metal pin badge and is limited to an edition of 50.

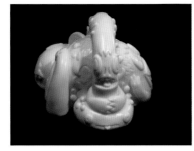

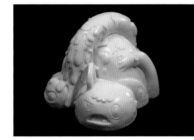

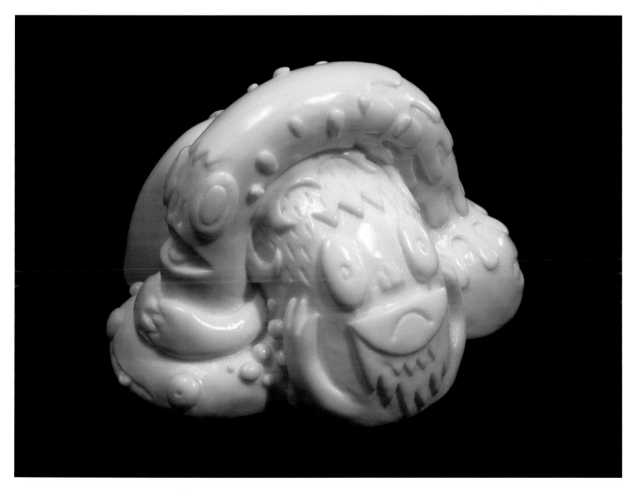

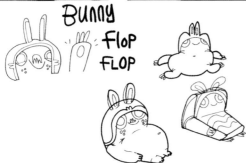

Bunny Flop

Bunny Flop is a collaboration with Martin Vicker of Medessin. Whilst knowing Martin for a long time we had never worked together before. When an exhibition focusing on collaboration came up we thought it would be a great opportunity to unite our disciplines for the first time.

Conceived in a back street alleyway (above Lee Rosy's tea room where they have great carrot cake) Bunny Flop is an Oldenburgian, soft-sculpture, bean-bag.

Many people in London, Nottingham and Manchester have experienced flopping out on his massive belly (shoes off first though) where up to three people can enjoy lounging around, whilst others can recline on his ample limbs.

1
Coasters
Drawings on cheap cork coasters.

2–5
Viva La Muralists
Interior doodle-orating at Common,
Manchester, in 2005, with messers
Neil 'Paris Hair' McFarland and Pete
'Monsterism' Fowler. Organised by
Doodlebug's Barney Barnes.

2

3

4

5

1
Nonpermanent and Secret Wars
February 17, 2007
Nonpermanent and Secret Wars
combined for an event at the Custard
Factory, Birmingham. Pete Fowler
and I 'battled' it out for an hour on
the canvases. It was not really a fight
though, we are not aggressive types,
it was more like a doodle-dosey-doe.

2
Latex Is Fun
Drawings on balloons for 'Latex Is
Fun' book and exhibition curated
by Max-o-matic.

6

11

7

8

12

13

9

10

1&2
Feel Good
Drawings on photos for a charity project and exhibition in Taipei organised by JustAnotherReason.

3
Yuck Collaboration
Print collaboration with Lille based artist and monster fan Yuck.

1

2

1–4
Street Signs
Project by Kanardo and Unchi,
on the streets of Lyon, France.

5
Stickers
In a variety of locations, some
more obvious than others.

1–10
Black Convoy
Black Convoy is a collective of illustrators and artists, formed in 2004, based around the UK. The capricious group collaborates either as a whole or in small fractions from time to time.

Current members include: Andy Potts, Neasden Control Centre, Austin Cowdall, Lee Ford, Mark Taplin, Adrian Johnson, Gary Neill, Tim Marrs and Holly Wales. Previous members included: Richard May, John McFaul, Miles Donavan and Andrew Rae.

Computer Arts cover by Black Convoy (1). Exhibition at Seventeen, Shoreditch, London (2–4). Collaborations with Black Convoy members Lee Ford (9&10) and Adrian Johnson (5–8).

5

6

7

8

9

10

Meals I've made

A single gulab guman, it did not last long (1). The baked potatoes were re-heated in the toaster, making them hot and crispy again (2.) Imagine my surprise as the Virgin Mary appeared on my plate after I ate a salad one day (3).

Soupy noodles with chunks of tofu (4). Chick pea salad that looks like a face drawn by a child (5). Vegetarian Sushi seems a strange concept but is still very nice to scoff (6). I like salads (7). Even ugly salads are nice (8).

Salads make me smile (9). Guess the famous London landmark (10). I call this meal Curry Bum-Bums (11). A little pre-dinner snack (12). Super stodgy pasta pile up, it sat in my belly for a week (13).

This is a rice cake, which is a funny sort of cake as it is not laden sugar and nice things (14). Fingers of roasted sweet potato enliven this cheeky little dish (15). Couscous, like rice, but not quite as nice (16). I pitta the fool who does not like this (17). Labelling these is making me hungry, where is my lunch? (18).

Can you guess what the dark item is in this dish? (19), Check my Flickr account to find out, Flickr.com/photos/jonburgerman.
It is very difficult not to take a bite out of your lunch before taking a photo of it (20). Seaweed flavoured rice crackers are crunchy good fun (21).

Actually this dish made me feel a little queasy (22). If you want to draw good cartoons you need to eat food like they eat in comics (23). Finished? There is a lot of licking left to be done to that bowl (24).

Boiled egg, baked potato, veggie
sausages (all cold). Not the
greatest packed lunch ever, but
at least it covers the much needed
brown and white food groups (1).

Zingy salad featuring beetroot
and goats cheese (2).

Meals I've enjoyed on my travels (not made by me)

Worryingly vibrant orange juice and chewy croissant in Riccione, Italy (1). Birthday thali and the now closed Veg Pot. Someone (Tristan) stole all the puddings and ate them whilst locked in the toilet. Greedy swine! (2). Chips and salad at Carringtons in Nottingham, near the train station (3). I forget what this once was (4).

Food on a ferry? Eat as much as you like? Four hours to kill? Well, ok then! (5). Filling up on the ferry (6). Feeling sick but still managed to squeeze down tinned pineapple, chocolate mouse and rice crispies (7). Spicy delights in Bazaar in Amsterdam (8).

Super nice quiche thingy in Rotterdam (9). Scone in 60 seconds… (groan) (10). After a drink or two I often see ladies paddling in my glass, enticing me in like Sirens… (11). Whatever this was I can guarantee it was not healthy (12).

Breakfast in New York with unlimited Bloody Mary's (13). A Singaporean breakfast treat; runny eggs with lashings of soy sauce and buttery toast, certainly different to my usual bowl of bran flakes (14). Following a healthy salad I enjoyed this lemon drizzle cake (15). Amazing character cookies made by a visitor to the Free Lunch show (16).

Dutch Dan is a Gooner and should not be encouraged (17). Goodies from my Free Lunch scam, I mean, exhibition (18). Pasta in a box at Analogue Books. We bumped into Spud from Trainspotting at the pasta shop, who was not on smack thankfully. It seemed he had matured a lot over the last few years (19).

Vegetarian food in Germany often means the same food as everyone else, just with the meat removed from one side of the plate (20). Truffle pasta in Dusseldorf (21). Food so fresh it's still on the chopping board (22). A nice British snack enjoyed in Paris (23). Scramby eggs and asparagus is a yummbles way to start a day (24).

Mock meat delights in Singapore, everything looks like it's been slaughtered but really it is just gluten (1). Noodles in Beijing, my first meal on Chinese soil (2). Dinner in Beijing, I think the brown stuff contained fish… eep (3). Strange but yummy vegetables in China, I wish I knew what they were (4). Burp (5). Tea and cake made by Greg in my studio in Nottingham (6).

Limp salad and bland white bap from one of the many poor sandwich shops in Hockley, Nottingham (7). Double O heaven, tea and toffee donut in London (8). Nuts, fruits (including passion fruit) and sandwiches, a good buffet stash (9). Salad bar goodness in Barcelona (10). Who took a bite of my pudding? (11). Deep fried and veggie, ticking all of my boxes in Singapore (12).

I love PieMinister pies and ate about four of them over a weekend at a music festival in Ireland (13).

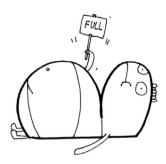

1

2

3

wee-pot

1–3
Wee-pot
Collaboration with knitting expert
Flo Harrison. Weepot is a cheeky,
incontinent pot, who always has a
smile and something hot brewing up
inside to share with you.

4
Grumpy Hats
Grumpy Hats makes its wearer very
grumpy indeed, as shown here by
this normally, very mild mannered
model. Feel the grumpiness coming
straight off the page directly at you.

4